AF134317

# PEGASUS ENCYCLOPEDIA LIBRARY

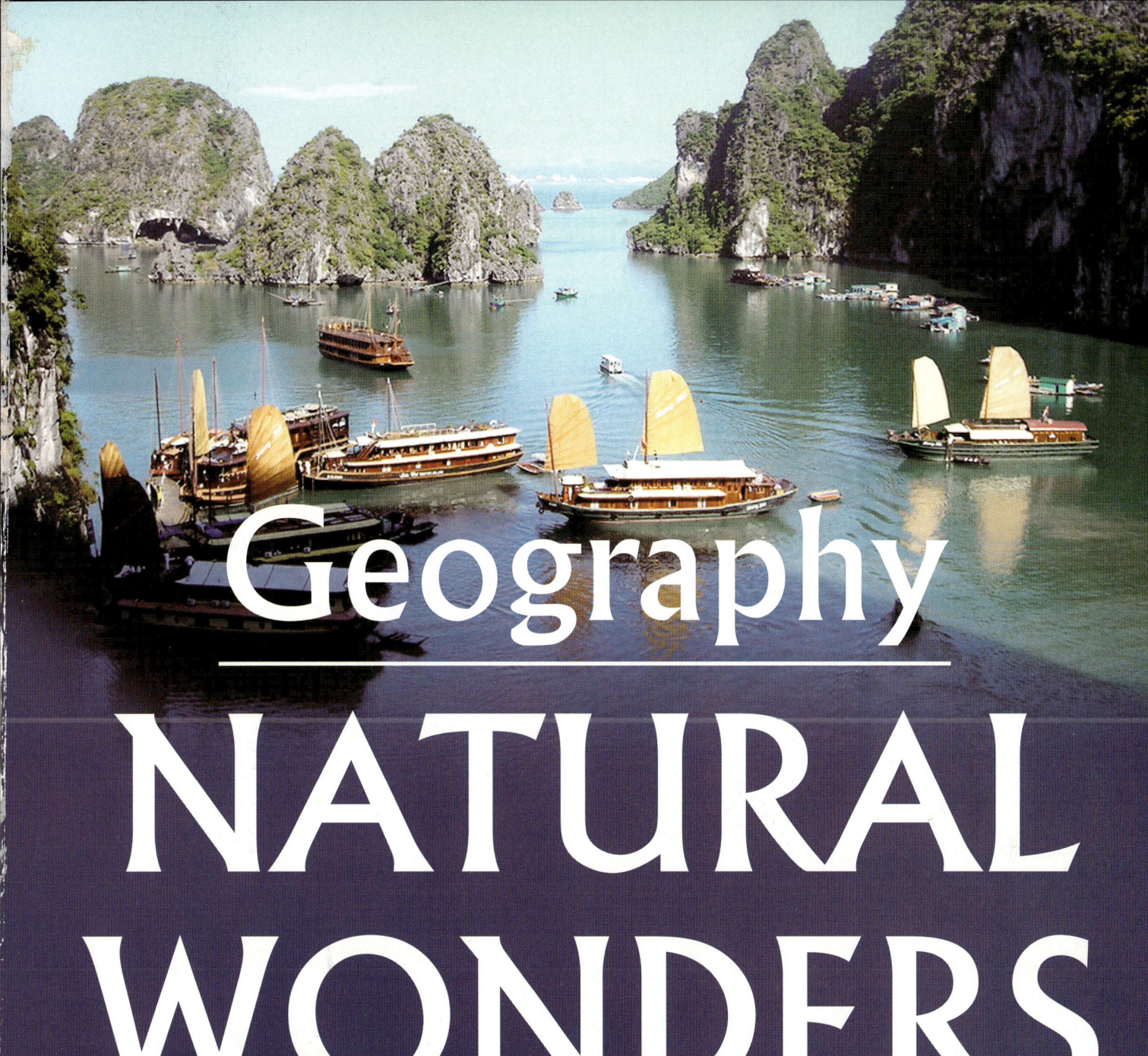

# Geography
# NATURAL WONDERS

Edited by: Pallabi B. Tomar, Hitesh Iplani
Managing editor: Tapasi De
Designed by: Vijesh Chahal, Anil Kumar, Rohit Kumar
Illustrated by: Suman S. Roy, Tanoy Choudhury
Colouring done by: Vinay Kumar, Kiran Kumari & Pradeep Kumar

NATURAL WONDERS

# CONTENTS

Amazing nature .................................................................. 3

Natural wonders of the world............................................... 4

Africa ................................................................................ 13

Asia .................................................................................. 17

Europe .............................................................................. 20

North America ...................................................................23

Oceania ............................................................................ 26

South America .................................................................. 29

Test Your Memory ............................................................. 31

Index ................................................................................32

# Amazing nature

Who amongst has not enjoyed looking at a beautiful sunset or a sunrise! We all have at some point of time stopped to admire a snow covered landscape or a beautiful sunny day. Nature truly is wondrous. It delights us, mesmerises us and at times surprises us. '**Natural wonders**' is a list of such natural events and places which arouse in us a feeling of awe and appreciation.

Though a limited list of natural wonders would not do justice to the extent of creative beauty and variety of Nature, an attempt has been made to present some of the most uniquely attractive natural places and events.

The first seven natural wonders in this book are the ones selected by CNN in the year 2007. The search for the new **Seven Wonders of the World** is still going on. But that should not stop you from knowing about some of the most amazing sites on our planet.

NATURAL WONDERS

# Natural wonders of the world

## Aurora Borealis

Aurora, also known as northern and southern (polar) lights or aurorae, is a natural display of coloured lights in the sky usually observed at night on both southern and northern hemispheres. It appears as a rippled curtain, pulsating glob, travelling pulse, or a steady glow of colourful light in the sky. It is seen in colours as different as blue, violet, red, ruby, bright green and yellow. The phenomenon occurs at higher altitudes with its lower most ends at 90 to 112 km above the surface of the Earth.

**Aurora borealis** is the name given to the aurorae occurring in the northern hemisphere. Aurora that is seen in the southern hemisphere is called **aurora australis**.

## How is it formed?

The core of our planet is made up of various metals which act like a giant magnet creating a magnetic field around the Earth called the **magnetosphere**. It extends far into space. An aurora is formed when electrically charged particles from the sun get pulled in and get trapped in the Earth's atmosphere due to Earth's magnetic field. These particles collide with the gases present at the poles giving off energy in the form of heat and coloured light.

Different gases produce different colours when they collide with these charged particles. For example, nitrogen causes red and blue aurora, hydrogen causes red aurora and oxygen causes blue and green colours. Since there is quite a bit of oxygen in the Earth's atmosphere, most aurora are a greenish blue colour.

Aurora borealis was named in 1621 by Pierre Gassendi, a French philosopher, priest, scientist, astronomer and mathematician, after the Roman goddess of dawn, Aurora, and the Greek name for north wind, Boreas.

Natural wonders of the world

# Grand Canyon

A canyon (also known as a gorge or a ravine) is a very deep valley with extremely steep sides, usually formed by the eroding action of a fast-flowing river that may or may not still be in existence.

The Grand Canyon is one of the largest canyons in the world, formed over billions of years by the Colorado River cutting into it. It is situated in the United States in the state of Arizona. It is 466 km long and approximately 29 km wide. The average depth of the Grand Canyon is 1,524 m and it covers about 1,218,376 acres of land area. The deepest part of the canyon is 1,829 m deep.

Even though the Grand Canyon is not the biggest canyon in the world, it is known for its beautiful and complex landscape made up of rocks of different hues and stunning colours.

It is a very important location for scientists who study the formation of our planet because of the thick sequence of old and ancient rocks beautifully preserved and exposed in the walls of the canyon. These rock layers record much of the early geologic history of the continent of North America over at least 2 billion years showcasing one of the most complete records of geological history in the world.

The Grand Canyon is one of the most popular wonders of the world attracting more than 5 million travellers every year.

## Astonishing fact

The Grand Canyon emergency rescue services save about 250 people who get stuck in the canyon due to exhaustion or injuries every year.

NATURAL WONDERS

## Paricutin Volcano

Paricutin Volcano is situated in the city of Paricutin which is located 320 km west of the Mexico City. The volcano erupted on February 20, 1943. Ashes from the Paricutin reached distances as far away as Mexico City! It is the fastest growing volcano ever recorded in history. It grew up to 45 m in just six days and 3,170 m in just 9 years.

The Paricutin Volcano is special because its birth and formation was witnessed by humans. On February 20, 1943, Dionisio Pulido, a farmer, was in his field preparing it for sowing. Suddenly, he felt a thunder rocking the ground beneath him and the trees started shaking too. Then he saw one of the most amazing (and terrifying!) event ever experienced by a human being—the birth of a volcano. The ground nearby opened in a crack of about 46 m length. Slowly the ground was raised 2 m in height and along with it smoke or fine dust like ash began to rise. The event was also accompanied with hissing and whistling sounds which were loud and continuous. A volcano had just born right under a farmer's feet...

Pulido and the rest of the farmers fled. By the next morning, nearby villages Paricutín (after which the volcano was named) and San Juan Parangaricutiro were both buried in lava and ash; the residents had relocated to a vacant land nearby. When the farmers returned to the site, the head of the volcano had grown to a height of 10 m and was throwing out rocks with great fury.

Even though this was one of the most violent volcanic activity ever observed and that too from such a close distance, no one was killed from the eruption itself but three deaths were reported that day from lightening strikes!

The volcano had grown 336 m tall in just one year. For the next eight years the volcano continued erupting. It stopped erupting in the year 1952.

## Victoria Falls

The Victoria Falls (locally called Mosi-oa-Tunya—the smoke that thunders') is a waterfall located in southern Africa on the Zambezi River between the countries of Zambia and Zimbabwe. The whole river drops headlong from a height of 108 m spanning the full one-and-a-half kilometre width of the river.

The Victoria Falls is neither the highest nor the widest waterfall in the world, it is however the largest. This claim is based on a width of 1,708 m and height of 108 m which forms the biggest curtain of falling water in the world and also one of the Seven Natural Wonders of the World. Victoria Falls is roughly twice the height of North America's Niagara Falls and more than twice the width of Horseshoe Falls.

The fall is so great that the spray from the falls normally rises to a height of over 400 m and sometimes even 800 m. Close to the edge of the cliff, spray shoots upward like inverted rain! This spray is visible from up to a distance of 50 km.

When David Livingstone, the famous Scottish missionary and explorer, the first European to discover the falls, first saw the falls, he said '...it (Victoria Falls) has never been seen before by European eyes, but scenes so wonderful must have been gazed upon by angels in their flight.' He named the falls in honour of Queen Victoria. His heart still lies buried in Africa.

At full moon, a 'moon bow' can be seen in the spray instead of the usual daylight rainbow. During the flood season, it is impossible to see the foot of the falls and most of its face, since the area around the falls is shrouded in mist.

NATURAL WONDERS

## Mount Everest

Mount Everest is the world's highest mountain above sea level with a height of 8,848 m. It is located in the Himalayan Range of mountains on the Nepal-Tibet border. Everest was named after an ex-British Surveyor General of India, Sir George Everest.

The tag of being the highest mountain in the world attracts many experienced mountaineers as well as amateur climbers who want to experience the joy of being at the top of the world, literally! The

Before Mount Everest came to be accepted as the highest peak, Kangchenjunga was considered to be the highest peak in the world.

Himalayas are the youngest mountain range on our planet and Everest was formed about 60 million years ago when the Indian sub-continent collided with Asia.

However, the Himalayas are still growing. They grow approximately 2.4 inches higher every year. 2.4 inches

does sound like a small figure but if one calculates it means that in the last 26,000 years the Himalayans have risen almost a mile into the upper reaches of the Earth's atmosphere!

It is interesting to note that until 1852 Everest was not considered the highest mountain on Earth. It was only in 1852 when Radhanath Sikdar, an Indian mathematician and surveyor from Bengal, stationed at the survey's headquarters in Dehradun first identified Everest as the world's highest peak. Even after that the official announcement that Mount Everest was the highest was delayed for several years due to verification procedures.

The first persons to climb the mountain successfully were Edmund Hillary and Tenzing Norgay in 1953. A large number of people have climbed Mount Everest after that and over 200 climbers have died in their attempt. A blind person, a one-legged person and a 70 year old have climbed the mountain successfully. The youngest person to climb Mount Everest was a 13-year-old boy named Jordan Romero in May, 2010.

The fact that Mount Everest is 97 degrees below freezing point is enough to give an idea about the difficulty of the climb. Most of the peaks in the Himalayas are permanently covered with snow. They do not melt even in the summers. Mount Everest is covered in a layer of ice all the year round.

NATURAL WONDERS

## Great Barrier Reef

A reef is a chain of rocks lying at or near the surface of the sea. A **barrier reef** is one which grows at some distance from the shore and has a lagoon (a small body of shallow water located near the sea shore) which separates the reef from the shore. Ocean reefs form underwater and are usually made up of coral, rock or sand. The top of the reef is positioned at two to three feet below the surface.

The Great Barrier Reef, located in the Coral Sea, near the coast of Queensland in Australia, is the world's largest reef system. It is made up of more than 2,900 individual reefs and 900 islands extending over 2,600 km and covering an area of approximately 344,400 km². It creates a natural water break between the immense waves of the Pacific Ocean and the coast of Australia. It is larger than the Great Wall of China!

The reef first became known to Europeans in 1770 when Captain James Cook accidently ran his ship in the region.

The Great Barrier Reef is blessed with the breathtaking beauty of the world's largest coral reef. It is made up of billions of tiny organisms called **coral polyps**. A polyp attaches itself to a rock on the sea floor and then starts dividing into clones. These organisms produce calcium carbonate forming a hard structure on which they live. The Great Barrier Reef is the world's largest natural collection of corals. Four hundred coral species, both

Natural wonders of the world

hard corals and soft corals are found on the Great Barrier Reef.

The reef contains an abundance of marine life. More than 1500 species of tropical fish, 200 types of birds, 20 types of reptiles, 30 species of whales, dolphins, and porpoise and six species of sea turtles have been recorded on the reef.

The reef was declared a World Heritage Site in 1981.

NATURAL WONDERS

## Harbour of Rio de Janeiro

The Harbour of Rio de Janeiro is located on the south-western shore of Guanabara Bay, which is surrounded by the city of Rio along a strip of land between the Atlantic Ocean and the Sugar Loaf Mountains, Corcovado Peak and the hills of Tijuca. The harbour was formed as a result of the eroding action of the Atlantic Ocean along the coast. Rio de Janeiro is the capital city of the State of Rio de Janeiro and the second largest city of Brazil.

The Guanabara Bay is the largest bay in the world based on volume of water. A **bay** is an area of water mostly surrounded by land but with a wide mouth, affording access to the sea. Bays generally have calmer waters than the sea due to the surrounding land blocking some waves and often reducing winds.

Rio (or the Guanabara Bay) bay is a natural wonder because of its scenic beauty and the illusions the place produces when one looks at it. The first explorers of the place thought it was the mouth of some giant river! This resulted in the naming of the place as Rio de Janeiro which means 'River of January'. The huge mountains which surround it make it seem like a lake. Some of the mountains are low and run straight into the water.

The beauty of the place is so great that it has often been said, 'God made the world in six days and on the seventh day he made Rio.'

# Africa

## Sahara Desert

The Sahara Desert located in the continent of Africa is the largest hot desert in the world extending over 9,400,000 square km, and the second largest desert overall (Antarctica is the largest desert in the world including hot and cold deserts). It covers most of Northern Africa, making it almost as large as Europe or the United States!

The Sahara Desert stretches from the Red Sea in the east, to the Atlantic Ocean in the west, the valley of the Niger River in the south to the Mediterranean Sea in the north. It covers 11 countries in its expanse — the countries of Algeria, Chad, Egypt, Libya, Mali, Mauritania, Morocco, Niger, Western Sahara, Sudan and Tunisia.

The landscape of the desert includes huge sand dunes and dune fields. It almost gives an appearance of a sea of sand.

NATURAL WONDERS

## Avenue of the Baobabs

The Avenue or Alley of the Baobabs is a group of baobab trees which stand along the dirt road between Morondava and Belon'i Tsiribihina in western Madagascar. Its visually captivating landscape attracts tourists from all over the world, making it one of the most famous locations in the area. A dozen trees about 30 m high of the species **Adansonia grandidieri**, which is only found in Madagascar, lie along the road. Those Baobab trees which are more than 800 years old are locally called '**renala**' which means 'mother of the forest'.

These trees were once part of the thick tropical forests that were once part of the geography of Madagascar. The forests were cut down for agriculture as the population of the country grew. Only the baobab trees, which the locals protected as sacred trees and also as a valuable food source and building material remained standing.

# Serengeti Migration

The Serengeti region in north-western Tanzania, extending up to south-western Kenya and covering some 30,000 square km, hosts the largest and the longest migration in the world, which is why it is one of the natural wonders.

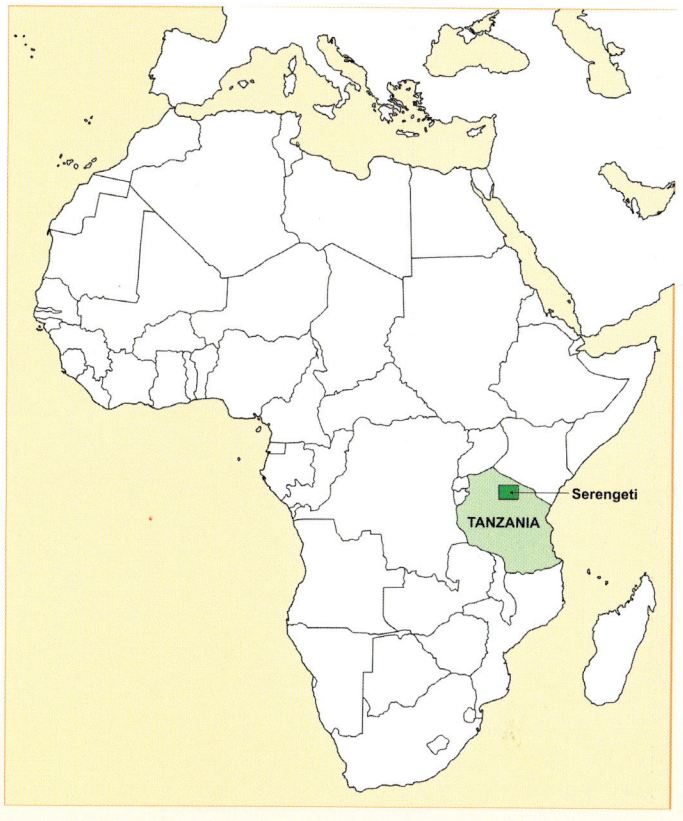

During the month of October, when the rains have stopped and the plains have dried out, almost 2 million herbivore animals (animals which feed mostly on grass and plants) along with the wildebeest move south in search of food and rains. The migration then moves on to the west towards Lake Victoria following the rain. With the start of the monsoon rains in December the wildebeest move back into the green Serengeti plains of Masai Mara. This phenomenon is sometimes called the '**circular migration**'. These animals use the widespread resources of the region in order to survive.

However, the journey is done not without some loss, some 250,000 wildebeest die during the journey from Tanzania to Masai Mara. Their migration is as old as the history of mankind. For many millenniums the wildebeest have followed the rains and have used the Serengeti with its patterns of grasslands to their advantage.

NATURAL WONDERS

## Table Mountain

Table Mountain is located in the Western Cape in South Africa. It is 1,087 m high. It stands over Cape Town and the Table Bay. The amusing thing about it is that the top of the mountain is not pointed like a peak rather it is flat like a table.

Sometimes a dense white mist covers its top and gives an appearance of a tablecloth. According to a local myth this happens because of a smoking contest between the devil and a local pirate called Van Hunks. The appearance of the tablecloth indicates the ongoing contest!

The Table Mountain is believed to be one of the oldest mountains in the world. It has over 1,500 species of plants, more than those found in the entire United Kingdom! The Table Mountain is a source of pride and income for the people of Cape Town and it features on their flag.

A 65-passenger cable car runs from Tafelberg Road to the top of Table Mountain. The floor rotates as it moves forward giving everyone a 360 degree view on the way up. The cable cars take about 5-10 minutes to reach the top of the mountain. Till date the cableway has transported more than 19 million visitors to the summit! 8,00,000 visitors from all over the world use the cableway annually.

Another interesting fact about the Table Mountain is that it is the only land feature to give its name to a star constellation (a group of stars in the sky that takes a recognizable form). The constellation is called Mensa, which means 'the table'.

# Asia

## Dead Sea

The Dead Sea is not really a sea! It is actually a salt lake lying on the borders of Jordan in the east, and Israel in the west. It is the lowest point on the surface of the Earth. Its surface and shores are 422 m below sea level! It is also one of the world's saltiest bodies of water; it is 8.6 times more salty than the ocean with a salinity of 33.7 per cent. With a depth of 378 m it is the deepest salt lake of the world.

Due to the presence of high quantities of salt, animals are unable to survive in this sea. That is why it is called the Dead Sea. It is 67 km long and 18 km wide at its widest point. The sea is fed mainly by the Jordan River. It has no outlet; therefore all water which reaches here does not go out as a river to any other place. The world's lowest road, Highway 90, runs along the Israeli and West Bank shores of the Dead Sea at 393 m below sea level.

Its water contains more than 35 different types of minerals that are essential for the health and care of the body and the skin including magnesium, calcium, potassium, bromine, sulphur, and iodine. They are well known for relieving pains and sufferings caused by arthritis, rheumatism, psoriasis, eczema, headache and foot-ache, while nourishing

### Astonishing fact

The Dead Sea was one of the world's first health resorts. King Herod the Great used to visit the sea for its health benefits

and softening the skin. They also provide the raw materials for various cosmetic products marketed worldwide.

### Astonishing fact

Anyone can easily float for hours on the surface of the Dead Sea without any danger of sinking because of natural buoyancy. One can easily recline on the water to read a newspaper.

NATURAL WONDERS

## Chocolate Hills

The Chocolate Hills are strangely coloured hills in the region of Bohol, Philippines. There are about 1,776 hills covered with grass spread over an area of more than 50 square km. During the dry season, the rainfall is so inadequate that the grass dries up and turns chocolate brown, giving the hills their colour and the name. The Chocolate Hills are a famous tourist

attraction of Bohol. They are featured in the flag and the seal of Bohol.

Various legends explain the formation of the Chocolate Hills. In one of them two giants quarrelled with each other by throwing rocks, boulders, and sand at each other. The fighting lasted for days, and made the two giants weary. In their tiredness, they forgot about their fight and became friends. But when they left they forgot to clean up the mess they had made during their battle. The mess later became the Chocolate Hills.

In one of the romantic legends, a giant named Arogo fell in love with Aloya, a mortal. Aloya died and as a result Arogo suffered much pain. He shed tears in his sorrow which when dried, formed the Chocolate Hills.

Asia

## Puerto Princesa

The City of Puerto Princesa is located in the south-west of Manila in Philippines. It is famous for the longest crossable and the most beautiful underground river in the world. It is 8.2 km in length and it moves through a beautiful cave before emptying into the South China Sea.

The river flows directly into the sea and the lower portion of the river is subject to tidal influences. According to a folk legend, the name 'Puerto Princesa' comes from a princess-like woman who is said to have roamed around the place on certain nights of the year.

NATURAL WONDERS

# Europe

## Blue Grotto

Capri Blue Grotto, known as 'Grotta Azzura' in Italian, is a world famous natural cave located on the Isle of Capri. It is famous for its magical, shimmering, intense blue tones and the magical silvery light which comes from the objects immersed in its waters. The effect is created by the daylight coming into the cave through an underwater opening located below the entrance of the cave. The light is filtered by the water which absorbs the red tones, leaving only the blue ones to pass into the cave. A visitor who puts his hand in the water can see it 'glow' eerily in this light.

In order to enter the Grotta Azzurra, visitors climb aboard small rowing boats, with a capacity for two, maximum three, passengers. The entrance to the cave is very small, about 1 m high above the sea level, and visitors are required to lie down in the boat while the boatman rows the boat inside through the passage. The inside of the cave has an average height of 7 m.

The Capri Blue Grotto has been known since ancient Roman times, especially under the rule of Emperor Tiberius. The remains of statues of the sea God Neptune dating to the first century A.D. have been found in the Grotto and they once lined the walls of the cave decorating Tiberius' private swimming pool. After Roman times the cave was avoided by locals, who believed it to be inhabited by witches and monsters.

# Eisriesenwelt Cave

The Eisriesenwelt (which is a German word for 'world of the ice giants') is a natural limestone ice cave located in Werfen, Austria inside the Hochkogel Mountain in the Alps. It is the largest ice cave in the world covering more than 42 km. It is visited by about 200,000 tourists every year. However, only the first kilometre, the area that visitors are allowed to visit, is covered in ice. The rest of the cave is made up of limestone.

In the Eisriesenwelt, the corridors and the cracks in the walls of the cave connect lower lying entrances to higher openings, hence making it possible for air to circulate in the cave. Depending upon the outside temperature, it is either warmer or cooler inside the mountain and this causes the air to circulate upwards or downwards. In winter, when the air inside the mountain is warmer than outside, cold air rushes into the mountain and reduces the temperature of the lower areas of the caves to below freezing point. In spring, the snow on the mountains melts and water seeps in through the cracks and freezes, slowly turning into the ice formations visible inside the caves.

These formations survive throughout the year because of the inflow and outflow of air. In winter, cold air blows into the caves, freezing the water that dripped into the cave during the warmer months. In summer, a cold breeze flows toward the entrance from deep within and prevents the ice from melting.

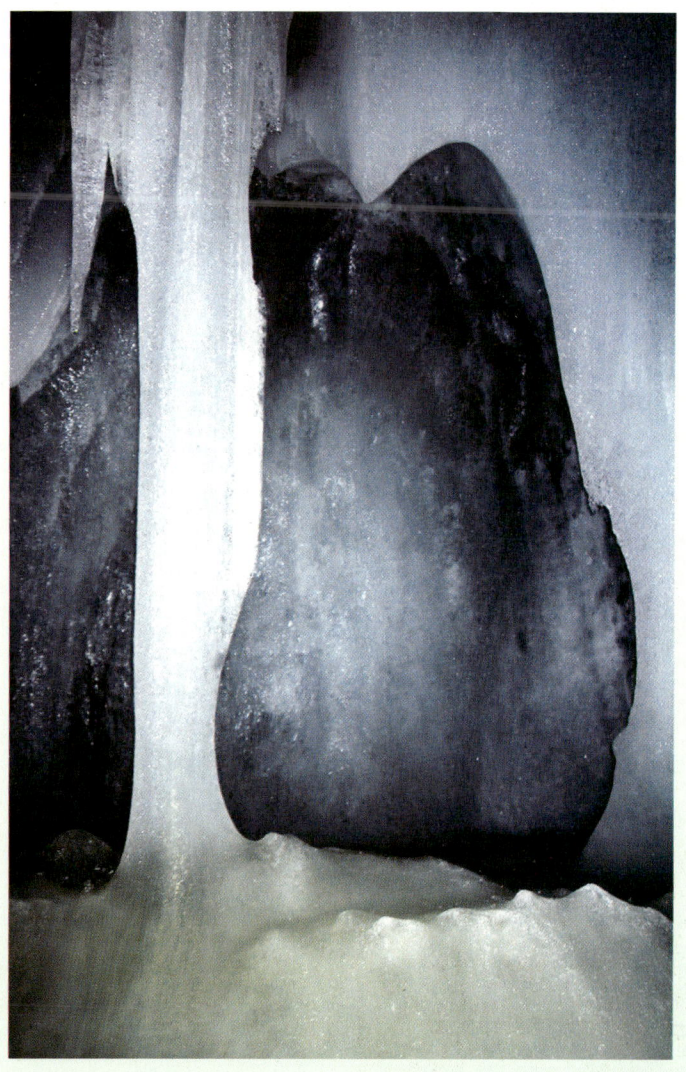

NATURAL WONDERS

## Azure Window

The Azure Window is a natural arch with a table-like rock over the sea in the Maltese island of Gozo. It was created millions of years ago when two limestone caves collapsed.

The arch of the Azure Window is, however, slowly disintegrating. Large

pieces of rock keep falling from the arch. It is expected that the arch will completely disappear within just a few years. The arch is in a dangerous condition and warning notices have been placed to stop people from walking over the top of the arch. Once the arch has completely crumbled away, the Azure Window shall be renamed Azure Pinnacle.

# North America

## Yellowstone National Park

The Yellowstone National Park is the first national park of the world formed on March 1, 1872. It is located in the United States of America in the states of Wyoming, Montana and Idaho. The park is known for its wildlife and its many geothermal features, especially the Old Faithful Geyser.

The Park covers an area of 8,980 km$^2$ including within lakes, canyons, rivers and mountain ranges. The Yellowstone Lake is one of the largest high-altitude lakes in North America and is located over the Yellowstone Caldera, the largest super volcano in the continent. The caldera (a large crater caused by the violent explosion of a volcano that collapses into a depression after the explosion) is considered an active volcano; it has erupted tremendously several times in the last two million years. The crater is almost 1 km deep.

Half of the world's geothermal features (relating to the heat present inside Earth) are present in the Yellowstone Park. Lava flows and rocks from volcanic eruptions cover most of the land area of Yellowstone. Yellowstone National Park has one of the world's largest forests covered by trees which were long ago buried by ash and soil and transformed from wood to mineral materials.

The most famous geyser in the park, and perhaps the world, is the Old Faithful Geyser, located in Upper Geyser Basin. It erupts 'faithfully' after about every 65 minutes for about 4 minutes, which is how it got its name. Castle Geyser, Lion Geyser and Beehive Geyser are also located in the same area. It also has the largest active geyser in the world—the Steamboat Geyser. In total there are 300 geysers in Yellowstone alone.

The name 'Yellowstone' comes from the Yellowstone River, which in turn gets its name from the yellow coloured rocky cliffs located on its banks in the northern region of the park.

The Earth's crust which is typically 32 to 50 km deep is only 3 to 4 km thick in most of Yellowstone.

### Astonishing fact

Since many areas of the Yellowstone park are located on fault lines, Yellowstone experiences about 2,000 earthquakes each year.

Grand Prismatic Spring in Yellowstone Park

# Great Blue Hole

A blue hole is a submarine cave or underwater sinkhole. They are also called vertical caves. They are roughly circular, steep-walled depressions, and so named for the stark contrast between the dark blue, deep waters of their depths and the light blue colour of the shallow waters around them. Since they are almost closed from all sides, the water circulation in such holes is poor, and they usually have low levels of oxygen after a certain depth.

The Great Blue Hole is a large underwater sinkhole off the coast of Belize. It lies near the centre of Lighthouse Reef, 70 km away from the mainland. The hole is circular in shape, with a diameter of over 300 m and a depth of 124 m. The blue cave is perfect spot for divers because of its beauty.

## Natural Bridge

Ever seen a bridge? Well, here's one too. But the amusing thing about this bridge is that it is completely a natural bridge. The Natural Bridge Virginia was completely made by nature and no human being was involved in its construction! It is a natural rock formation in the shape of an arched bridge located in Virginia in North America.

The bridge is actually part of the remains of the roof of a cave or a tunnel through which Cedar Creek, a small tributary of the James River, once flowed. The Bridge forms an arch at the height of 66 m with a span of 27 m. With such a huge size it belittles and at the same time bemuses its visitors.

The Bridge was once a sacred site of the Native American Monacan tribe. The name of the town that the bridge is located in is also Natural Bridge, located in the Rockbridge County.

The third president of the United States, Thomas Jefferson, on seeing the bridge said that it was 'the most sublime of nature's works'. The U.S. Highway 11 runs across the bridge.

NATURAL WONDERS

# Oceania

## Ayers Rock

Uluru, also called Ayers Rock, is an 'island mountain', an isolated leftover after the slow erosion of a large mountain range located in the southern part of the Northern Territory, central Australia. It is a large sandstone rock and is one of the oldest rocks on Earth with most of its bulk below the ground. It was formed over a period of about 500 million years!

Uluru is famous for appearing to change colour as sunlight strikes it at different times of the day and year from different angles. The sunset is a particularly remarkable sight when the rock briefly glows red in colour. Although rainfall is uncommon in this area, whenever it rains the rock acquires a silvery-grey colour.

The local people call it Uluru. This word has no particular meaning in their language. Uluru is sacred to the Aboriginal people of the area. Aborigines (a person, animal, or plant that has been in a country or region from earliest times) think of it as a symbol of all creation.

A myth tells of two tribes of ancestral spirits who were invited to a feast, but did not show up. To take revenge, the angry hosts put an evil spell into a mud sculpture that came to life as a dingo (a wild or half-domesticated dog with a sandy-coloured coat, found in Australia). There followed a great battle, which ended in the deaths of the leaders of both tribes. The Earth itself rose up in grief at the bloodshed, becoming Uluru. It is believed that those who take rocks from the mountain will be cursed and suffer misfortune.

On July 19, 1873, a surveyor named William Gosse discovered the mountain and named it Ayers Rock in honour of the then-Chief Secretary of South Australia, Sir Henry Ayers.

## Ross Ice Shelf

Ice shelves are thick plates of ice, formed continuously by glaciers, which float on the surface of an ocean. These ice shelves act as 'brakes' for the glaciers preventing them from moving too fast into the ocean.

The Ross Ice Shelf is one of many such shelves. It is the largest body of floating ice in the world with an area of roughly 487, 000 km$^2$, about the size of France. It is several hundred metres thick. The nearly vertical ice front to the open sea is more than 600 km long, and between 15 and 50 m high above the water surface. 90 per cent of the floating ice, however, is below the water surface. In some places, the ice shelf can be almost 750 m thick. The Ross Ice Shelf pushes out into the sea at the rate of between 1.5 m to 3 m a day.

Sometimes fissures and cracks may cause a part of the shelf to break off. The largest known break-off was about 31,000 km$^2$ which is slightly larger than the size of Belgium!

The ice shelf was named after Captain James Clark Ross who discovered it on January 28, 1841.

**The world's largest iceberg**

Iceberg B-15 is one of the world's largest recorded icebergs. It is 295 km long and 37 km wide. With an area of over 11,000 km$^2$, it is larger than the island of Jamaica. It is so huge that even after almost a decade parts of B-15 have still not melted. It was formed out of the Ross Ice Shelf in March, 2000.

An iceberg is a large piece of ice that has broken off from a snow-formed glacier or ice shelf and is floating in open water.

NATURAL WONDERS

## The Pinnacle Desert

The Pinnacles are limestone formations located within Nambung National Park, near the town of Cervantes in the Pinnacles Desert, Western Australia. Thousands of huge limestone pillars rise out of a landscape of yellow sand. At some places they reach up to a height of three and a half metres. Some are jagged, sharp-edged columns, rising to a point while others resemble gravestones.

The raw material for the limestone of the pinnacles came from sea shells created by marine organisms. These shells were broken down into lime-rich sands which were brought ashore by waves and then carried inland by the wind to form high, mobile dunes. The Pinnacles are thus the eroded remnants of the formerly thick bed of limestone.

# South America

## Amazon Rainforest

The Amazon Rainforest, also known as the Amazonia or the Amazon Jungle, is the world's largest tropical rain-forest. It covers five and a half million square km. About 60 per cent of the rainforest is within Brazil, 13 per cent in Peru and some parts in Colombia, Venezuela, Ecuador, Bolivia, Guyana, Suriname and French Guiana. The Amazon is over half of the planet's remaining rainforests.

The forest is home to about 2.5 million types of insects, tens of thousands of plants, and some 2,000 birds and mammals. At least 40,000 types of plant, 3,000 types of fish, 1,294 types of birds, 427 types of mammals, 428 types of amphibians, and 378 types of reptiles have been scientifically identified. One in five of all the birds in the world live in the rainforests of the Amazon.

It is often claimed by the scientists that one square kilometre of Amazon forest may contain more than a thousand types of trees and thousands of species of other higher plants. Amazon rainforest birds account for at least one third of the world's bird species. The number of edible fruits found in the rainforest is estimated to be about 3,000.

### Astonishing fact

The forests have been named 'the lungs of the planet' since they produce more than 20 per cent of Earth's oxygen.

NATURAL WONDERS

## Angel Falls

Angel Falls (locally known as Kerepakupai vena, meaning 'waterfall of the deepest place', or Parakupa-vena, meaning 'the fall from the highest point') is the world's highest waterfall, with a height of 979 m and the longest uninterrupted drop of 807 m. The waterfall drops over the edge of the Auyantepui Mountain in the Canaima National Park in Venezuela. They are about 20 times higher than Niagara Falls.

The waterfall was named after Jimmie Angel, a US pilot who was the first to fly over the falls in a plane. The Angel Falls was unknown to Venezuelans until the early 1930's. Without the invention of the aeroplane the Venezuelans might not have ever found Angel Falls. The falls are only accessible by a boat or an aircraft because of steep slopes and thick jungle surrounding them.

The water of the falls appears to be coming from a flat-topped plateau called Auyan-Tepui, which means 'Devils Mountain'. The fall is so tremendous that people walking within a radius of 1.6 km may get sprayed with mist coming from the waterfall during certain times of the year.

# Test Your MEMORY

1. In which hemisphere does Aurora Borealis occur?

2. In which hemisphere does Aurora Australis occur?

3. Who is the Roman Goddess of dawn?

4. Which gas in the atmosphere causes red aurora?

5. Which river is responsible for the formation of the Grand Canyon?

6. What is the name of the volcano whose birth and formation was witnessed by a Mexican farmer Dionisio Pulido in 1943?

7. What is the local name for Victoria Falls?

8. How many countries does Sahara Desert cover in its expanse?

9. What is the lowest point on the surface of the Earth?

10. What is the name of the first national park of the world?

11. Which famous rock formation or 'island mountain' is known to change colours according to the angle of sunlight that falls on it?

12. What is the name of the world's highest waterfall?

NATURAL WONDERS

# Index

**A**

Amazon Rainforest  29
Angel Falls  30
Aurora australis  4,
Aurora borealis  4,
Ayers Rock  26
Azure Window  22

**B**

bay  12, 16
Blue Grotto  20

**C**

caldera  23
canyon  5,
cave  19, 20, 21, 24, 25
Chocolate Hills  18
cliffs  23
coral polyps  10

**D**

Dead Sea  17
desert  13, 28
dune  13

**E**

Eisriesenwelt Cave  21

**G**

geyser  23
glaciers  27
Grand Canyon  5
Great Barrier Reef  10, 11
Great Blue Hole  24

**I**

iceberg  27

**L**

lagoon  10

**M**

magnetosphere  4
mountain  8, 9, 12, 16, 21, 23, 26, 30
Mount Everest  8, 9

**N**

Natural Bridge  25
Niagara Falls  7, 30

**P**

Paricutin  6
Pinnacles Desert  28
polar  4

Puerto Princesa  19

**R**

rainforest  29
reef  10, 11, 24
Ross Ice Shelf  27

**S**

Sahara Desert  13
sand  10, 13, 18, 28
Serengeti Migration  15

**T**

tropical rain-forest  29

**V**

Victoria Falls  7
volcano  6, 23

**W**

waterfall  7, 30

**Y**

Yellowstone National Park  23

---

\* Maps not to scale; for illustration purpose only.